# DEDICATIONS

## TOM GOODLET

This book is dedicated to my smoking hot wife, Erica, who is constantly supporting new ventures and teaching me to be slower to speak and quicker to chase wisdom. I also want to thank and recognize those who have been encouragers and mentors to me in my adult life like Donnie, Jay, Kurt, Ray, Pop, and most of all Mom and Dad.

## MATT GARDNER

I dedicate this book to my beautiful wife and best friend, Emily, and to my mother and father for always being there to support me, and to Frank, Ryan, Nick, and Tom for truly being my mentors.

# contents

# ACKNOWLEDGMENTS

Thank you Jodi Costa for doing all the work and giving everyone else all the credit.

Bob Reed, Sherry Prewitt, Christie Dittmer and Debbie Willeson for doing the research and letting us bounce ideas that would later shape MentorU

Jonathan Adrian for letting us chase seemingly crazy ideas to see if they work.

Harborside Christian Church people for trying this out.

Ryan Bailey, Ron Carlson and Angie Appleget for proofing.

Adrian Traurig for photography.

Sarah Castle and Lisa Miller for helping the whole Team succeed.

Jared Kidwell for letting us try this stuff out and giving great feedback.

Saddleback, Willow Creek and Southeast Christian Church for paving the way.

**WELCOME** to the life-changing adventure that is MentorU. Before you get started, here are some tips on how to best use this tool. That's right, MentorU is a tool. This means that the tool should never trump the user, but rather the user should always trump the tool. Use MentorU in a way that best meets the Mentor's and Mentee's needs. If you don't like a question, then don't use it. If you have a better way to describe something then use your definition. If you want to change the order, skip a part, spend more time on one area, add or take away some homework, then do it. You won't hurt our feelings. We just want to help get a mentoring relationship started.

**Tip 1:**
Get at least one book for the Mentor to use, and a separate book for the Mentee. This way both participants can take their own book home, look ahead or review the material, and keep notes and answers that are pertinent to each individual.

**Tip 2:**
Ask lots of questions. Yes, we have loaded this material with questions, because that is how we believe we often learn best. Jesus often taught His followers by asking questions, and it got them thinking. If one written question spurs on another unwritten question, ask it. Tangents are ok with us. Let the conversation go where it must. We trust you to get it back on track when the time is right. Also, we would especially encourage the Mentee to prepare questions outside of the material for their Mentor to answer. This ensures the vast wealth of knowledge available from the Mentor to the Mentee is not hindered by questions we forgot to ask in the MentorU curriculum.

**Tip 3:**
Use the blank lines under the questions to fill in your own answers, but also feel free to use them to write some of the other person's answers. This can especially help the Mentor remember details occurring in the Mentee's life. You may also use the space to jot down notes, thoughts and questions for future reference. Decide when you want to write in your answers to questions. Some participants would rather answer the questions ahead of time so they can spend the majority of the session time sharing the answers they have already thought through. Other participants would rather reduce the amount of work outside of the session and answer each question on the fly while going through the material during the mentoring session. Whichever works best for you is the one you should choose.

**Tip 4:**
Build patterns in your session times together. Each session contains certain recurring questions or time segments we believe are important to your ongoing growth and relationships. For example, we think it is always important to take a moment and see how each individual is doing. A lot can happen between sessions. It's good to talk about it and gauge the mood of each participant before you move forward. We would also strongly suggest you reserve time to answer questions not in the material. You should take time to talk about subjects that are important to you. We also think that it is important to build prayer time into each session and write down the topics. It is always amazing to see God at work, but sometimes you can miss it if you don't write it down. There are other recurring questions and sections in each session. We put them there because we think they're important. We encourage you to use them no matter what ongoing learning material you are using.

**Tip 5:**
Take your time. MentorU is divided into six sessions, but that does not mean it has to stay that way. Once you decide how often you are going to meet, you can start working your way through the material. Unless you are on some crazy time crunch, we suggest you take as little or as long a time as you need to cover and digest each part. There is no rush. You may only cover one part of one session when you meet. That is okay.

**Tip 6:**
Enjoy the moments. We know not all mentorships last a lifetime. In fact, most mentorships last a season. That is okay, because this meaningful time was what was needed during that season. So enjoy the season. Learn as much as you can and enjoy the time you have together. As you grow it is okay and often necessary to adjust. So don't feel bad about it. It usually means you are doing something right. Everything great has a starting point and often a stopping point. Think of your growth plan as a step-by-step process rather than set path. Measure each step, take each step, and let God guide the rest. Enjoy the journey!

# introduction

## Why Mentorship?

The word "mentor" was first recorded in the ancient writings of Homer, specifically in the story of Odysseus. In this story, Odysseus embarks on a perilous journey and leaves his son at home under the care of a trustworthy friend named, "Mentor."

Mentor serves as a wise counselor and advisor to the young man, guiding him into the future on a journey of his own. As a follower of Jesus, we are also traveling on an epic journey of faith and service to God, gaining wisdom and experience along the way.

Mentorship is the opportunity for an individual to share his or her wisdom and experience with someone else who needs it. Mentors share their knowledge, insights, and skills in order to instill value from himself or herself into someone else. When Jesus called his disciples to come and follow Him, He was inviting them into a personal and significant opportunity for growth. These men were able to watch and learn from Jesus, storing up His wisdom in their hearts.

Following the example of Jesus, the disciples then took what they learned and experienced, instilled it into a new generation of leaders, repeated the process, and passed on a wealth of knowledge to those who followed after.

Jesus did it. While Jesus spent much of His time with the crowds, He spent most of His time pouring into a few individuals.

so, why mentorship?

Mentorship is a vehicle by which valuable knowledge and experience impacts the life of future generations. Without it, each generation is bound to experience the same mistakes and limitations as the one before it. There is no progress, no growth. That being said, the result of a healthy mentorship is personal progress and deeper growth. In the life of the Mentee, he or she will receive insight, guidance, encouragement, and accountability from someone with more life experience. They are able to absorb that knowledge and experience and then expand on it in their own life, providing exponential growth in their future. In the life of the Mentor, he or she will experience new growth through the practice of "discipling." We tend to be fed more when we are feeding. Mentoring someone will provide more opportunities and experiences that fill up each individual involved. It is important to know that either position, Mentor or Mentee, has the incredible potential of growing your heart and mind to be more like Jesus.

*MentorU is a universal first step*

*that identifies an individual's next step*

**WHO SHOULD BE MY MENTOR OR MENTEE?**
You are in the best position to select and decide who should be your Mentor or Mentee. We want to equip you with some questions that will increase your chances of success. We want to help you make a **CLEAR** choice.

who should I mentor?

who should be my mentor?

someone who ...

someone who ...

**EASILY CONNECTS**
With whom do I have chemistry?
With whom do I naturally bond?

**EASILY CONNECTS**
With whom do I have chemistry?
With whom do I naturally bond?

**IS A LEARNER**
Who wants to, and makes steps to learn?

**IS A LEARNER**
From whom can I learn?

**IS EXCITED**
Who brings an energy, motivation,
and/or drive with them?

**IS EXCITED**
Who brings an energy, motivation,
and/or drive with them?

**IS AUTHENTIC**
Who is real with him/herself and
honest with you?

**IS AUTHENTIC**
Who is real with him/herself and
honest with you?

**IS RELIABLE**
Who will show up, invest and participate?

**IS RELIABLE**
Who will show up, invest and participate?

We encourage you to seek out someone who models a Christ-centered life. Your Mentor should possess fruitful life experiences that you desire to see in your own life – that may be in their faith, their marriage, or maybe how they raised their children. Your Mentor should have the kind of experience and reputation that would make you want to become more like them.

# HOW TO START:

**step one** — pick a time, place & frequency

**step two** — swap communication info & send a reminder

**step three** — meet

MentorU is a journey for a Mentor and a Mentee to take together.

Both Mentor and Mentee should both answer as many questions within the curriculum as are appropriate.

## HELPFUL TIPS

Here are some thoughts and helpful tips for your mentoring journey:

> *"Mentoring is not a race. If you run fast and try to finish first, you'll finish alone."*
>
> – John Maxwell – Five Levels of Leadership

Our transient nature and the desire for instant gratification can often place pressure on the mentorship process. Realistic goals and a steady relationship are important for a healthy mentorship.

> *"Be imitators of me, as I am of Christ." 1 Corinthians 11:1 ESV*
>
> – The Apostle Paul

We do not have all of the answers, nor can we take all the credit for our success. A healthy mentorship places Christ as the final authority of truth and the provider of the blessings in our lives.

Mentors should be careful not to impose their personal goals and visions on their Mentee. The highest goal is for the Mentor is to help the Mentee seek God's guidance for their life and become more like Christ. So Mentors should use their knowledge and experience as a resource and not a strict guideline.

Mentoring relationships are open relationships. Mentors, be encouraged to share the stories of your life and not just the principles which you live. Mentees, be honest about your dreams and ask questions. (Bringing questions for your Mentor to each session is encouraged.)

> *"Life is short, but there is always time enough for courtesy."*
> – Ralph Waldo Emerson

It is important to be courteous of each other's time and effort in this relationship. Be clear in your communication, be timely, demonstrate appreciation, hold confidentialities, extend grace and encourage each other. These are just a few ways to bring mutual support and consistency to your mentorship relationship.

> *"Deeper spiritual growth comes with intentional life adjustments."*
> – Tom Goodlet

In order to dive deeper into what God has planned for your life, there will be at least two life adjustments required. This mentorship tool will promote both a relational adjustment and an attitude adjustment.

## 1. RELATIONAL ADJUSTMENT:

We need to move from a group setting to a one-on-one relationship.


## 2. ATTITUDE ADJUSTMENT:

We need to move from a "What can I get?" to a "What can I give?" frame of mind.

# - 1 -

# yoUr story

## How is it going?

You made it to your first meeting! You should thank each other for showing up and for being willing to begin this process. Start with your hopes and expectations for the mentorship:

What made you interested in starting this mentorship?

_____

_____

_____

Where and when is the best time to continue meeting?

_____

_____

_____

Do you have any ideas or guidelines you would like to share?

_____

_____

_____

_____

How do you want to grow during this time?

_____

_____

_____

_____

For your first session together the focus will be on yoUr STORY.

# What is it?

Everyone has a story. Every story is important. Within these stories, we find a window into the life of another person. We are able to discover the paths, experiences, circumstances, decisions, adventures, failures, and tragedies that have formed the person in front of us into who they are today. Our past is important. It not only defines who we are today, but also helps us connect to others in ways we may have never expected. The mentorship journey is all about moving forward. If you want to move forward with someone then you need to know where they came from.

If you don't feel like a you are great storyteller, don't worry too much about this one. No one knows your story better than you do. So let's give it a try. Take turns sharing the answers to the following [yoUr story] questions:

Where did you grow up?

_____

_____

What was your family like?

_____

_____

_____

Where did you go to school?

_____

_____

_____

What was your first job?

_____

_____

_____

Who have been the most influential people in your life (good or bad)?

_____

_____

If you are in a relationship, describe its origins.

_____

_____

_____

Where does Jesus fit within your story?

_____

_____

_____

_____

_____

_____

_____

# Why is it important?

Sharing your story is a building block for a strong and healthy mentorship. For a moment, think of all the different pieces of your past that have come together to dramatically impact your present day life. Those real experiences are tools. They are mentorship currency, and when shared in telling your story, they will create personal opportunities for growth, encouragement, and empathy.

In the Bible, we see a powerful example of mentorship in the relationship between Paul and Timothy.

**READ Acts 22:2-21**

With the knowledge you have and the information from this passage, how would you answer the previous [yoUr story] questions on Paul's behalf?

_____

_____

_____

_____

_____

Paul was a harsh and violent religious leader in the Jewish community when he experienced a life-changing encounter with Jesus Christ on the road to Damascus. This moment changed every aspect of who Paul was: it changed his heart, his mission, and even changed his name (formerly Saul). Paul was setting out on his second missionary journey when he met a young man named Timothy.

**READ Acts 16:1-4 and 2 Timothy 1:1-4**

With the knowledge you have and the information from this passage, how would you answer the previous [yoUr story] questions on Timothy's behalf?

_____

_____

_____

_____

_____

Timothy grew up in a home with a Jewish mother and a Greek father. We do not know what happened to Timothy's father but it seems that he is not really active in the life of this family anymore, and may possibly be deceased or separated from the family. Timothy and his mother were both followers of Jesus when Paul came to their city. Timothy had gained a reputation in the community for his godly heart and character.

These two men had very different stories, but what they learned about each other brought them together and changed both of their lives forever. Paul found someone who shared his heart and passion for spreading the message of Jesus around the world. Timothy found someone who had experienced a lot of growth and a lot of change. Paul was someone he could learn from and look up to – a healthy and consistent father figure.

# Where do we go with this?

Sharing your story is important because it builds connection and trust with your mentorship partner. It is part of what makes you, you. If you are going to grow and move forward in your story then you must first understand yourself. Each of you share your present story:

Where do you live?

_____

_____

What does your family look like?

_____

_____

_____

What is your work situation?

_____

_____

_____

What are your hobbies and interests?

_____

_____

_____

How do you feel emotionally today (tired, excited, depressed, hopeful, etc.)?

_____

_____

_____

At this time in your life, what is most important to you?

_____

_____

_____

What are your current Spiritual habits (ex. reading the Bible, praying, journaling, fasting, tithing etc.)?

_____

_____

_____

On a scale of 1 to 10 how close do you feel to Jesus? Why?

_____

_____

_____

_____

Do you see any correlations from the story of your past intersecting with your current life story? Explain.

_____

_____

_____

_____

What are your dreams for the future?

_____

_____

_____

What are your concerns for your future?

_____

_____

_____

Where do you find hope?

_____

_____

_____

# How do we move forward?

**HOMEWORK:** Between now and the next time you meet, take time to continue to explore what makes you, you.

Take time to do a personality profile and a spiritual gifts assessment. Here are a few suggestions and resources for these tests.

You will discuss the results for Mentor and Mentee at your next session.

SpiritualGiftsTest.com
A free online survey with definitions and descriptions for results

**Wired that Way**
Purchase this survey at
CBD.com or Amazon

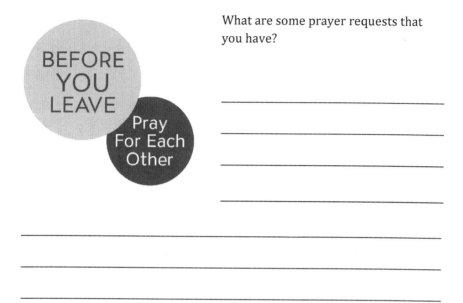

BEFORE YOU LEAVE

Pray For Each Other

What are some prayer requests that you have?

_____

_____

_____

_____

_____

_____

_____

# - 2 -
## yoUr design

## How is it going?

Welcome to the second session. After doing your homework, hopefully you discovered even more details to yoUr story. For example: discovering how God has wired you. Before digging into the results of your homework, start answer a few questions:

Is there anything else you would like to share regarding your story that you did not share last time we met?

_____

_____

_____

What events have happened in your life since the last session?

_____

_____

_____

How are your friends and family?

_____

_____

_____

Where have you recently seen God at work?

_____

_____

_____

What have you been learning about yourself?

_____

_____

_____

For your second session together, the focus will be on yoUr DESIGN.

# What is it?

It is time to look a little deeper into your DESIGN. Sound scary? Well do not fear; you won't be sharing your darkest secrets, shouting your imperfections or talking about your body type. Your previous mission was to share your story – giving an account of the external situations and influences of your life. Your DESIGN is very different. This is the internal content of your heart, soul, and mind. Here is what your DESIGN means:

**D**esires
the dreams and passions that drive your life

**E**xperience
the knowledge formed from your past
interactions and observations

**S**kills
your developed talents and natural abilities

**I**deals
the values and beliefs that influence
the choices you make and teach

**G**ifts
the Spiritual gifts that God works within you

**N**ature
your prewired personality and character
traits that determine how you best operate

These six key components help identify who you really are and how God has gifted you to impact the world around you. Most people have a general feeling of what their DESIGN is like, but many have not taken the time to clearly define these parts of themselves.

Take the time now to answer questions regarding your **DESIGN**:

# Desires – What do you get most excited about? What gets your blood pumping? What are you passionate about? What would you love to do more often if you were able? What do you want to accomplish, achieve or create in the next 5 to 10 years?

_____

_____

_____

_____

_____

# Experience – You have already shared your story. What are three things you have learned as a result of your past?

_____

_____

_____

_____

_____

**Skills** – What are your top talents?  What abilities come naturally to you?  What skills are you developing?

_____

_____

_____

_____

_____

**Ideals** – What is most important to you? When you look at the world around you, what breaks your heart or makes you angry?  Who or what do you tend to fight for?  What beliefs or values do you have that are unwavering?

_____

_____

_____

_____

_____

**Gifts** – According to the Spiritual Gifts test you took, what are your three top spiritual gifts? Do you agree with the test results?  Why?

_____

_____

_____

_____

_____

**Nature** – According to the Personality Profile test you took, what type of personality, or mixture of personalities are you? Do you agree with the test results?  Why?

_____

_____

_____

_____

_____

# Why is it important?

Have you ever tried to use a spoon to cut a steak? While you may experience some rate of success, you determine the spoon was not designed to cut meat. Of course you can have a similar experience if you try to eat peas with a knife. The point is, understanding how and why something or someone is designed is critical information. It is not only about figuring out if you are a spoon, knife or maybe even a fork, it is also about finding your place at the table, so to speak.

Knowing your personal and  purposeful design brings clarity to your individual purpose but it also reveals your place within the greater design. You are a part of a bigger picture. You are not alone.

Everyone who has ever worked on a picture puzzle understands that not every piece fits together. Additionally two pieces that are designed to fit together will not find their proper relationship unless the pieces are correctly lined up.

Clearly identifying your design will help you discover two things: how you can better understand and connect to another person and how your piece fits into the bigger picture of God's Kingdom.

While some parts of our DESIGN are continually developing and have the freedom to change and adjust (Desires, Experience, Skills, Ideals), there are some parts of your DESIGN that are more set and outside of your choice and control (spiritual Gifts, Nature, natural Skills). Your nature and natural skills are pre-wired by God, and your gifts are distributed by God. There are no bad personalities and no bad spiritual gifts. These are intentional parts of God's design. God is a God of purpose so we know that there is purpose to His design for you.

**READ Ephesians 2:10.**

What descriptions identify you in this passage?

_____

_____

_____

What purpose is defined for you according to this passage?

_____

_____

_____

When discovering the good works God prepared for you to do, it is important to consider each part of your DESIGN. For the remainder of this session, focus simply on one part, your pre-wired Nature or personality.

When thinking about the major relationships in your life, which natures /personalities do you see in the people around you? Explain.

_____

_____

_____

Are there certain personalities you get along with more than others?

_____

_____

_____

# Why is it important?

This simple idea still reigns true: personalities are different. You shouldn't underestimate the power of using this knowledge to lead and relate to others better.

Among the disciples of Jesus, there were many different natures /personalities. Jesus interacted differently with John than He did with Peter. Jesus had a very close relationship with both men, inviting them to be a part of special moments during His time on earth (*Matthew 17:1-9; Mark 5:37-42; Mark 14:32-36*). Peter's personality would fall more into an impetuous and proactive nature, and John's would be a milder and more reactive nature.

How do we see Jesus respond?

**READ Matthew 16:21-23 & John 18:7-11**

When Peter was assertive and outspoken, how did Jesus respond?

_____

_____

_____

**READ John 13:21-25; John 21:7 and John 21:20-24**

John was young and gentle by nature. So what do these verses indicate about the relationship that Jesus had with John?

_____

_____

_____

Who do you more relate to in nature – John or Peter? How do you feel God most often compliments or compensates for your personality?

_____

_____

_____

# Where do we go with this?

Whether you are more like a Peter or a John God has a purpose for your personality. God uses every personality in leadership. God uses everybody who is willing, to do good works.

What do you think God was thinking when He began to create you?

_____

_____

_____

Do you think there are any of your gifts, passions or experiences that have gone to waste? Explain.

_____

_____

What do you think God is telling you as you discover more about yourself?

_____

_____

_____

How do you think understanding ourselves might affect how we approach others? Explain.

_____

_____

_____

Knowing your story and your DESIGN better are good starting points for identifying your next step for following Jesus.

# How do we move forward?

Between now and the next time you meet, think about how you might use your DESIGN to follow Jesus. Think of people who are wired similar to you and consider what they are doing with their lives. Look for other tests and ways to better identify how you are wired.

Share what you are learning about yourself with those closest to you.

**HOMEWORK:** For your next meeting, write down three ways you think God has used you in the past:

_____

_____

_____

_____

List three ways you think He might use you in the future:

_____

_____

_____

_____

**BEFORE YOU LEAVE**

**Pray For Each Other**

What are some prayer requests that you have?

_____

_____

_____

_____

_____

_____

_____

# - 3 -
## yoUr reality

## How is it going?
How are you really doing?

_____

_____

_____

Where have you recently seen God at work?

_____

_____

_____

Do you have any questions for your Mentor or for the one you are mentoring?

_____

_____

_____

_____

_____

Welcome to the third session. After doing your homework, hopefully you discovered and confirmed even more details regarding your DESIGN.

**DISCUSS THE RESULTS OF YOUR HOMEWORK:** Share with each other three ways you think God has used you in the past and three ways you think He might use you in the future.

Are there any patterns you see throughout the course of your life? Explain.

_____

_____

_____

Do you see any purpose behind how God has wired you? Explain.

_____

_____

_____

Do you notice any parts of your DESIGN keeping you from God? Explain.

_____

_____

_____

Do you notice any parts of your DESIGN drawing you closer to God? Explain.

_____

_____

_____

Since beginning this mentorship, do you perceive any messages God is sending you? Explain.

_____

_____

_____

For the third session together, the focus will be on yoUr REALITY.

# What is it?

More than likely, you have heard this phrase: "perception is reality". This idea has been around for a while; exhausting time and coffee supplies as individuals attempt to express reality as they experience it. So, give it a shot and discuss these questions:

"Perception is reality" - what does this statement mean to you?

_____

_____

_____

Can you recall a time when you were convinced of something but someone else was convinced you were wrong? Share.

_____

_____

_____

"Reality" is your interpretations, perceptions, motivations, and personal experiences that make up what you see, and how you experience the world around you. So when an event occurs, there are different interpretations and different accounts of what happened or who was responsible. Your reality is personal, it is intimate, and it feels very real. But the person sitting next to you may live with a different perception of reality. If you have ever watched sports, then you understand the referees officiating the game make calls and decisions that are disputed by the masses. With recent advances in technology, these disputes can often be settled by digitally reviewing the action to amend or affirm the referee's call made on the field. Here we find an important distinction between what the referees saw, what the angry fans saw, and what actually happened.

Do you find it difficult to see other people's perspective in a conversation or argument? Explain.

_____

_____

_____

Do you view things as "black and white" or is there room for personal interpretation in ethical or moral areas? Why or why not?

_____

_____

_____

So this is the heart of the conversation: there is a distinction between "perception of reality" and "actuality," between the way we see it and the way it actually is – the distinction between where we are and where we need to be. Perception of reality is always up for interpretation, but actuality is concrete, universal, and all-powerful. Jesus Christ, in all actuality, is Lord and Savior – how does that impact your reality?

The goal is to acknowledge that your actual reality must be constantly conforming to the image and power of Jesus Christ. While God loves us just as we are, He also loves us enough not to leave us this way.

> Your actual reality is that God
> is always trying to mold and
> make you more like Jesus.

# Why is it important?

Our reality changes all of the time, changing with the tides of circumstance and stability in life. Today, your reality may be succeeding in work or providing for your family. Tomorrow, may be discovering an illness or saying goodbye to a loved one. But what if your reality were firmly anchored on unchanging truth, God-given purpose, and unconditional love?

**READ Romans 12:1-2.**

What timeless truth is packed into these two verses?

_____

_____

_____

God has displayed His mercy by sending Jesus to pay the price for our sins, wiping away our debt and removing the fear of death. With this truth, your response and reality is to submit your life to God. The result is being able to "test and approve what God's will is" (NIV) – you are able to further apply actual truth to your life. The more you know and submit to God, the more your reality forms around Him.

**READ Proverbs 3:5-6.**

What do you think it means to submit to God?

_____

_____

Why do you think it is sometimes hard to submit to God?

_____

_____

_____

What internal area of understanding needs to submit to God?

_____

_____

_____

If you submit and trust in God, He will make your path straight. He will provide stability and clarity for your life. To go through life wrapped up in your own reality is to go through life apart from God. The personal allure of defining your own reality is getting to set your own rules, expectations, and values. The downside is that no one else cares, you are alone, the ruler in a universe of one person. We are instructed to lean not on our own understanding and to avoid conforming to the world around us. By opening our eyes to the actual truth of the Gospel, we connect ourselves to God and are connected to a body of believers.

## Where do we go with this?

Your reality is not about you. It is actually about Jesus. God is trying to make and mold us to be more like Jesus.

> It is not about you being a better you.
> It is about you being a better Jesus.

It is all about who you know, with whom you are connected, and whom you reflect.

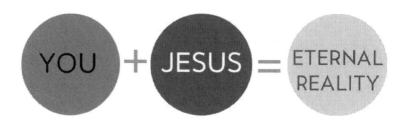

YOU + JESUS = ETERNAL REALITY

To blow the doors off your reality, add Jesus. Everything we lack is found in our Savior. Everyone needs to invest his or her self into knowing more about Jesus and becoming more like Him.

How do you think becoming more like Jesus is an ongoing process?

_____

_____

_____

How might you identify the next step in your process of becoming more like Jesus?

_____

_____

_____

What do you think of when you hear the word "discipleship"?

_____

_____

_____

A disciple is a student. Discipleship is the process of a student learning from a teacher in an effort to become more like the teacher. It is a process of replicating. It is a process of a student conforming to the mind and heart of his or her teacher. It is you becoming more like Jesus.

**Read Matthew 28:18-20**

According to this passage what makes a person a disciple of Jesus?

_____

_____

_____

It is time to embrace your reality. You are still here on this earth to follow in the footsteps of the Teacher. You are here to learn from Jesus so you can become more like Him, and guess what? We are all far away from being just like Him. There are so many areas where we lack compared to Jesus. That is why it is an ongoing process with tools like mentorship to aid in that development. Jesus is the standard of measurement. Realizing where you do not measure up to Jesus identifies your next step to work on in order to become more like Him.

While we will never match the perfection of Jesus (apart from Jesus), it is more about the pursuit and journey. The beauty and blessing of this pursuit is it does not matter that we fall short of Jesus because we all do. What matters is we love Him enough to learn from Him.

So are you ready to do what it takes to become more like Jesus?

## How do we move forward?

The goal is to acknowledge that Jesus Christ, in all actuality, is Lord and Savior. Your reality must be constantly conforming to the image and power of Jesus Christ.

**HOMEWORK:** For the next time together, each of you list at least ten things you know to be true about Jesus.

_____

_____

_____

_____

_____

_____

_____

_____

_____

_____

How do you know these attributes are true? Make an effort to attach Scripture to your list.

_____

_____

_____

_____

_____

_____

_____

_____

_____

_____

**BEFORE YOU LEAVE**

**Pray For Each Other**

What are some prayer requests that you have?

_____

_____

_____

_____

_____

_____

_____

## - 4 -
## yoUr relationship

## How is it going?
How are you really doing?

_____

_____

_____

Where have you recently seen God at work?

_____

_____

_____

Do you have any questions for your Mentor or for your Mentee?

_____

_____

_____

Welcome to the fourth session. After doing your homework, hopefully you discovered some more details regarding your reality.

**DISCUSS THE RESULTS OF YOUR HOMEWORK:** Share with each other the ten things you know about Jesus and how you know them to be true.

What are some of your favorite attributes about Jesus? Why?

_____

_____

_____

When looking at your life in comparison to the life of Jesus, how does it make you feel?

_____

_____

_____

What do you think God wants for your life as you learn more about the life of Jesus?

_____

_____

_____

How would you describe your love and level of commitment to Jesus?

_____

_____

_____

For the fourth session together the focus will be on yoUr RELATIONSHIP.

# What is it?
## Are you a Fan or a Follower?

In his book "Not A Fan," Kyle Idleman explores the difference between those who are fans of Jesus and those who are truly followers of Jesus.

He identifies a "Fan" as "an enthusiastic admirer." A fan will display His enthusiasm for his team by proudly wearing his favorite player's jersey on game day. You can't miss his loyalty because he has bumper stickers on his car or truck and on game day will proudly display his allegiance to his team by hanging a large team flag in front of his house. The enthusiasm of the fan comes to a zenith on game day when the fan is committed and focused while his team performs.

However, his level of commitment wavers throughout the performance if his team is not reaching the levels of expectation the fan requires for his ongoing devotion. In reality, the enthusiastic admirer's commitment is solely based on someone else's performance and not his own. Since the dedication to the team is subject to the performance by someone else, it may become common that the fan is only seasonal and is easily willing to dump the team as one would discard the trash on Monday morning.

Are you a Fan of Jesus? Do you root for Jesus from the stands? Explain.

_____

_____

_____

Is your commitment to Jesus seasonal? Does it change depending on the day of the week or the season of the year? Explain.

_____

_____

_____

Kyle Idleman, author of *Not A Fan*, defines "Follower" as "one who is guided or committed to following another person".
**READ Matthew 4:18-22**

How would you describe the disciples' response to Jesus' invitation?

_____

_____

_____

What other ways could they have responded?

_____

_____

_____

From what you know, what was the overall outcome of their response to following Jesus?

_____

_____

_____

Does Jesus give us a similar invitation?  Explain.

_____

_____

_____

By contrasting these definitions of a fan and a follower you begin to differentiate between those who only profess their faith in Christ and those who are willing to commit to His service. The fans are positioned on the sidelines to cheer on their Savior until they are challenged or sacked too many times, only to retreat to a defeated position. In contrast, the followers know they are offering themselves unconditionally.

How would you rate your commitment level to Jesus?

_____

Are you closer to being a fan or follower?

_____

How do you think those closest to you would rate you?

_____

Is there a difference between what you want to be and what you actually have been? Explain.

_____

_____

_____

What do you think drives commitment? What do you think makes it stronger? What do you think makes commitment important?

_____

_____

_____

_____

_____

# Why is it important?

Your reality is that God wants you to become more like Jesus, but...

> the question remains,
> "Do you really want to become
> more like Jesus?"

It is time to answer the question that comes up in every relationship. It is time to have the DTR (Define The Relationship) talk. This is the conversation that determines whether or not the relationship is going to move forward, and whether it has the potential to move to the next level.

**READ Matthew 16:13-19**

In this passage, what do you think sets Peter apart from the others?

_____

_____

_____

What does Peter bring to his relationship with Jesus?

_____

_____

_____

What does Jesus bring to His relationship with Peter?

_____

_____

_____

How does identifying their feelings about one another move the relationship forward?

_____

_____

_____

Do you think commitment is a feeling or an action?  Explain.

_____

_____

_____

Who is Jesus to you?

_____

_____

_____

What are you ready to bring to the relationship?

_____

_____

_____

> If you don't know where you stand today
> with Jesus, you won't be ready to follow
> His lead tomorrow.

So it is time to figure out where you stand with Jesus.

# Where do we go with this?

Define the relationship you want have with Jesus:

_____

_____

_____

What your the obstacles?

_____

_____

_____

What are your opportunities?

_____

_____

_____

What are your problems and challenges?

_____

_____

_____

What are your rewards?

_____

_____

_____

How close do you feel to Jesus today?

_____

_____

_____

What motivates you to follow Jesus?

_____

_____

_____

Do you think heaven will be heaven if Jesus is not there? Why?

_____

_____

_____

_____

**READ Matthew 25:31-46**

What stands out to you about in this passage?

_____

_____

_____

How do you know that you really know Jesus?

_____

_____

_____

How do you know that Jesus really knows you?

_____

_____

_____

Before you can move any further, you will have to decide. Do I want to be a sheep or a goat, a fan or a follower? Do I want people to know me or know Jesus?

It all comes down to a choice, because commitment is a choice, an ongoing choice.

> Jesus has already chosen the
> type of relationship
> He wants with you.

Now you get to choose the type of relationship you want with Jesus.

# How do we move forward?

Before the next session together, take time to contemplate and answer the following three questions:

**HOMEWORK:**
Who do I want to be?

_____

_____

_____

What will it take?

_____

_____

_____

What am I waiting for?

_____

_____

_____

BEFORE
YOU
LEAVE
Pray
For Each
Other

What are some prayer requests that
you have?

_____

_____

_____

_____

_____

_____

_____

## - 5 -
## yoUr plan

## How is it going?
How are you really doing?

_____

_____

_____

Where have you recently seen God at work?

_____

_____

_____

Do you have any questions for your Mentor or your Mentee?

_____

_____

_____


Welcome to the fifth session. After doing your homework, hopefully you discovered some significant details regarding your relationship with Jesus.

**DISCUSS THE RESULTS OF YOUR HOMEWORK:**  Share with each other your answers to the following questions:

*Who do I want to be?*
*What will it take?*
*What am I waiting for?*


For the fifth session together the focus will be on yoUr PLAN.

# What is it?

If you have accepted the reality that God wants to mold and make you more like Jesus, and you are ready to allow Him to do it, then it is time to begin the process of mapping out a plan.

The point of this plan will be to learn vital lessons from Jesus in order to become more like Him. The plan will help identify and map out your next steps. The end product will be a road map for a journey that the Mentor and Mentee will take together. Of course, this plan is subject to God's leading. So be prepared for Him to guide you as you map out each step.

This will also be an opportunity for each Mentor to specifically pour into the Mentee.


**READ 1 Corinthians 11:1**

Do you think Paul told Christians to follow him because he would do everything perfectly? Explain.

_____

_____

_____

What do you think you stand to gain from the successes and failures of your Mentor?

_____

_____

_____

The common thread of this mentorship experience should be a pursuit of Jesus. There are more than a lifetime of lessons to learn when following Jesus. For the sake of this mentorship experience, we simplified what you can learn from Jesus into three "how to" categories:

# Why is it important?

First, observe what you stand to gain if you focus on learning from Jesus in these three areas.

We will break down each area by definition, disciplines, and discoveries to be made.

## HOW TO LEAD LIKE JESUS

DEFINITION = *What does it mean?*
Leadership is influence. We are all called by God to be leaders at some level. Leading others is part of following Jesus' lead.

DISCIPLINES = *What are some ways Jesus did it?*
Read Mark 1:16-18 and Matthew 28:18-20. Write your thoughts.

_____

_____

_____

DISCOVERIES = *What can we learn from Jesus?*

We can learn ...

- How to influence the world for good.

- How to better communicate, problem solve, empower others, and evaluate opportunities and circumstances.

- How to be a leader and overseer within the local church.

- How to be a Mentor to someone else.

## HOW TO LOVE LIKE JESUS

DEFINITION = *What does it mean?*
God is love (1 John 4:8)
Love is the greatest attribute that we have to offer (1 Corinthians 13:13)
Jesus is our greatest example of what love looks like (John 15:13)

DISCIPLINES = *What are some ways Jesus did it?*

Read Matthew 22:35-40. Write your thoughts.

_____

_____

_____

DISCOVERIES = *What can we learn from Jesus?*

We can learn …

- How to love God with all your heart, soul, mind and strength.

- How to love others, including your spouse, kids, extended family, Christian and non-Christian friends.

- How to share the love of Jesus with those who do not yet know it.

**HOW TO LIVE LIKE JESUS**

To live like Jesus we must do what He did. Jesus practiced multiple spiritual disciplines. Perhaps your next step in mentorship is to consider implementing one new spiritual discipline into your life.

We chose to highlight seven disciplines of Jesus worth embracing. Each one will take time to develop because to live like Jesus is a PROCESS.

# Praying

DEFINITION = *What does it mean?*
It is conversation with God with the expectation of Him listening and speaking. It is more than time spent with God, it is time invested.

Oswald Chambers *(My Utmost for His Highest)* wrote: "We tend to use prayer as a last resort, but God wants it to be our first line of defense. We pray when there's nothing else we can do, but God wants us to pray before we do anything."

DISCIPLINES = *What are some ways Jesus did it?*
Read Matthew 26:36, Mark1:35, and Luke 5:16. Write your thoughts.

_____

_____

_____

DISCOVERIES = *What can we learn from Jesus?*

We can learn ...

- How to pray different types of prayers, like prayers of praise, of thanksgiving, confession (telling God we are sorry), supplication (asking God to help through provision), and intercession (asking God to help others).

- How to use different prayer styles, like devotional prayer(scripture based), spontaneous prayer (straight from the heart without much thought), contemplative prayer (long and thoughtful), and action prayer (while walking, working, or moving).

- How to journal prayer requests and answered prayer.

# Reading the Bible

DEFINITION = *What does it mean?*
It is taking time each day to read God's message, with the intention of it guiding the way you think and act.

DISCIPLINES = *What are some ways Jesus did it?*
Read Matthew 4:3-4. Write your thoughts.

_____

_____

_____

DISCOVERIES = *What can we learn from Jesus?*

We can learn ...

- How to build a habit where you set a time and place that allows you to focus as you read the Bible.

- How to select a Bible reading plan.

- How to journal for retention, including writing down what is interesting about the passage (observation) and writing how you can apply the passage to your life (application).

# Offering

DEFINITION = *What does it mean?*
It is giving back to God your "first-fruits," the first 10% or more of income with the intention of putting God first in your life and relying on His provision.

DISCIPLINES = *What are some ways Jesus did it?*
Read Matthew 22:20-21 and Mark 12:41-44

_____

_____

_____

DISCOVERIES = *What can we learn from Jesus?*

We can learn ...

- How giving can build our trust in God.

- How giving can build our testimony to share with others.

- How giving can build God's Kingdom.

- How giving can build blessings for yourself, and for others in your church, community, and around the world.

# Ceasing from Something

DEFINITION = *What does it mean?*
It is abstaining from something like eating (fasting) or noise and interaction (solitude) for a designated period of time with the intention of focusing on God's Will and His Word.

DISCIPLINES = *What are some ways Jesus did it?*
Read Matthew 4:1-2, Mark1:35, and Luke 5:16. Write your thoughts.

_____

_____

_____

DISCOVERIES = *What can we learn from Jesus?*

We can learn ...

- How fasting can put you in the best possible position for a breakthrough.

- How fasting can help you give up bad habits.

- How fasting and solitude can bring inner clarity and peace.

- How solitude can bring refreshment, restoration and healing.

# Engaging in the Church Body

DEFINITION = *What does it mean?*
It is prioritizing active participation within the local church, with the intention of worship and fellowship. You were not meant to go through life alone. Take your place within the body of Christ. Be a part of the bride of Christ, the hope of the world.

DISCIPLINES = *What are some ways Jesus did it?*
Read Luke 4:16. Write your thoughts.

_____

_____

_____

DISCOVERIES = *What can we learn from Jesus?*

We can learn ...

- How to be an essential part of a church family.

- How to truly participate in corporate worship.

- How to give and receive encouragement and accountability.

- How the local church can spur on spiritual growth.

# Studying Scripture

DEFINITION = *What does it mean?*
It is digging deeper into the words and meaning of Scripture in an effort to gain even greater understanding.

DISCIPLINES = *What are some ways Jesus did it?*
Read Luke 2:46-47 and John 7:15. Write your thoughts.

_____

_____

_____

DISCOVERIES = *What can we learn from Jesus?*

We can learn ...

- How to use biblical tools to better understand the meaning of words and the context of passages (author, audience, place, time, culture, customs, etc.).

- How to use and view Bible translations.

- How to memorize and meditate on Scripture in order to better understand and internalize the passages.


# Serving

DEFINITION = *What does it mean?*
It is dying to yourself. It is putting the desires of God and the needs of people before yourself.  As you become more like Jesus, He will challenge you to be more about others and less about self. Your growing love for God motivates you to increasingly love others. That is how it works.

DISCIPLINES = *What are some ways Jesus did it?*
Read Mark 10:45 and John 13:3-5. Write your thoughts.

_____

_____

_____

DISCOVERIES = *What can we learn from Jesus?*

We can learn ...

- How to evaluate your DESIGN and God's plans, and then minister to others in a way that reflects both.

- How to commit to giving a set-proportion of your time to do God's work.

- How serving can strengthen you and lead to significance.

- How you can be fed more when you are feeding.

## Where do we go with this?
What disciplines are present or absent in your life today?

_____

_____

_____



Would you rather strengthen something already present in your life, work on adding something new, or tackling a weakness? Why?

_____

_____

_____


## How do we move forward?

**HOMEWORK:** Before the next session together, take time to continually contemplate the previous questions. Both Mentor and Mentee should take time and prioritize each learning possibility above, primarily with the Mentee in mind. Be prepared to compare notes during your next time togheter. This should put both of you on a path to developing a good spiritual growth plan for the Mentee.

Which heading (Lead, Love or Live like Jesus) currently gets you the most excited?

_____

_____

_____

What are your top three discoveries you want to learn from Jesus?

_____

_____

_____

What is currently at the bottom of the list of what you want to learn from Jesus?

_____

_____

_____

BEFORE
YOU
LEAVE

Pray
For Each
Other

What are some prayer requests that you have?

_____

_____

_____

_____

_____

_____

_____

## - 6 -
## yoUr move

## How is it going?
How are you really doing?

_____

_____

_____

Where have you recently seen God at work?

_____

_____

_____

Do you have any questions for your Mentor or for the one you are mentoring?

_____

_____

_____

Welcome to the sixth session. After doing your homework, hopefully a spiritual growth plan is beginning to come into focus.

**DISCUSS THE RESULTS OF YOUR HOMEWORK:** Share the results of your homework with each other:

What were the top things you felt were most valuable to learn from Jesus?

_____

_____

_____

Why did you prioritize them the way you did?

_____

_____

_____

Which things do you think your Mentor will be best able to speak about due to his or her experience? Explain.

_____

_____

Are there any things not listed that you would both like to learn and improve upon? Explain.

_____

_____

_____

What have you enjoyed from this mentorship experience so far?

_____

_____

_____

What has been valuable learning information as a result of this mentorship relationship?

_____

_____

_____

Do you feel ready to move forward in this learning experience? Explain.

_____

_____

_____

While the initial steps in this Mentorship are universal, the next step needs to be tailored to the individual. In other words, everybody needs to share his or her story. Everybody needs to understand his or her DESIGN. Everybody needs to accept the reality that God wants to make us more like Jesus, commit to a relationship allowing Jesus to be the standard, and consider a plan conforming us into the image of Christ. However, the first step of the plan is different for everyone.

> You have to first identify the first step of the plan, and then you have to actually take it. It's your move to make!

## Why is it important?
**READ Matthew 21:28-32**

How would you retell this story?

_____

_____

_____

What might this story have to do with "Talking the talk and walking the walk?"

_____

_____

_____

To which one of these sons do you relate most? Why?

_____

_____

_____

Do you find any redeeming quality in understanding what is expected of you and yet are still not doing anything about it? Explain.

_____

_____

_____

**READ James 1:22-25**

How do you think this passage of scripture relates to the previous passage in Matthew?

_____

_____

_____

What are some things you have learned in this mentorship?

_____

_____

_____

What do you think are some expectations that will result from this knowledge?

_____

_____

_____

What do you think are some excuses that can get in the way of these expectations?

_____

_____

_____

The reality is that often the biggest obstacle in your way of growth and becoming more like Jesus, is you.

You may talk all day about what you should do or could do. You may even get excited thinking about what it might look like. However, if you never put any of those thoughts into actions, then it is wasted time.

# Where do we go with this?
**Map it out. Figure out your next step.**

Based on your previous prioritization, see if you can agree upon some of the additional steps after the completion of this initial curriculum. Choose a time for your next meeting.

What do you both agree that you should work on first when it comes to learning from Jesus?

_____

_____

_____

Take a moment to look at some curriculum options regarding your choice of next step at **www.MentorU.info**

Feel free to discuss and decide to use other books or curriculum outside of the listed resources. Lock in a choice for your next step. Order any materials needed to begin this next step.

Now, take a moment and celebrate! You did it! You took the time and invested effort to grow and go further on the journey with Jesus. We hope you enjoy your next steps on this exciting journey.

Thank you, Mentor, for your willingness to share.
Thank you, Mentee, for your vulnerability to grow.

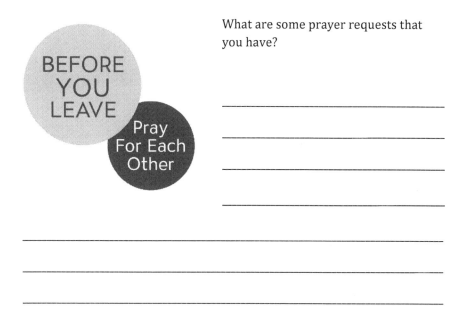

BEFORE
YOU
LEAVE

Pray
For Each
Other

What are some prayer requests that
you have?

_____

_____

_____

_____

_____

_____

_____

## THE NEXT STEPS IN OUR
## MENTORING RELATIONSHIP:

_____

_____

_____

_____

_____

_____

_____

_____

_____

_____

_____

_____

# references

1.  Maxwell, John C., *5 Levels of Leadership*, page 8

2.  ESV Version – 1 Corinthians 1:11, page 9

3. Emerson, Ralph Waldo, page 9

4. Idleman, Kyle, *Not A Fan*, page 45

5.  Chambers, Oswald, *My Utmost for His Highest*, page 57

# ABOUT THE AUTHORS

**Tom Goodlet** is a husband, a father and a forever student of Jesus Christ.

He is married to his beautiful wife Erica and has two boys, Parker and Mason, and a little girl, Avri. He is currently the Associate Minister at Harborside Christian Church in Safety Harbor, FL. Prior to taking this position he was in full time youth ministry for 11 years. Tom has a BS in Communications from Milligan College in East Tennessee and a Masters of Arts in Theological Studies from Liberty University. Tom grew up just outside of NYC in Hicksville (nothing hick about it), Long Island. Tom loves humor, adventure and Jesus.

**Matt Gardner** is a Student Pastor in Northeast Tennessee where he and his wife currently live. Matt studied student and church ministry at Liberty University in Lynchburg, VA and has since served the local church through his passion for Student Ministry.

Want more?
MentorUs. A Universal First Step that Identifies a Couple's Next Step.
www.MentorU.info

Made in the USA
Columbia, SC
20 January 2023

75508048R00043